AUSTIN C. LOVELACE

THE ORGANIST
AND
HYMN PLAYING

ABINGDON ⓐ PRESS

NEW YORK — NASHVILLE

107901

THE ORGANIST AND HYMN PLAYING

Copyright © 1962 by Abingdon Press

B

SET UP, PRINTED, AND BOUND BY THE
PARTHENON PRESS, AT NASHVILLE,
TENNESSEE, UNITED STATES OF AMERICA

FOREWORD

In an earlier book, *Music and Worship in the Church*,[1] a small section was devoted to hymn playing as being one of the most important jobs of the church organist. The material presented there was the nucleus for the more comprehensive treatment in this book. While the earlier presentation was designed to state the role of the organist not only to himself, but to everyone else in the church, the present work is specifically designed for the organist.

It is highly recommended that this book be studied —not skimmed through—with hymnal near at hand. Every principle and suggestion should be tried out and mastered so that it can be applied to other material.

I gratefully acknowledge permission from Abingdon Press to use material from *Music and Worship in the Church*.

It is hoped that this short treatise will help make more organists aware of the "awesome" responsibility that is theirs in leading the congregation in worship through the playing of hymns.

[1] Austin C. Lovelace and William C. Rice (Nashville: Abingdon Press, 1960).

CONTENTS

CONTENTS

CHAPTER I

Pedaling

Correct pedaling is the first step to good hymn playing, for any uncertainty—as to choice of heel or toe, or distances between notes—causes anxiety and nervousness which in turn creates mistakes in fingering, tempo, and interpretation. Organ playing requires that something be automatic, since the mind can concentrate only on so many things at once. Therefore, habitually correct pedaling is basic to good hymn playing.

All organ method books recommend that the bench be a comfortable distance from the keyboard so the toes clear the black notes by about an inch or so when the legs are hanging freely. If the bench is too close there is difficulty in moving easily from white to black notes; if the bench is too far back the organist has the sensation that he is about to fall on his face on the keys. The height of the bench should also be adjusted to let the balls of the feet touch flat on the white notes.

When the organist is seated in the middle of the bench the left foot should fall over C, second on the pedal board, and the right foot over E, two notes above. The purpose of this position is to give a point of reference to which the organist can always turn when confused about the location of notes. Most exercise books choose these notes as starting points from which all intervals are learned—by gliding the foot smoothly over one, two, three, or more notes to the correct interval of a second, third, fourth, et cetera.

In actual practice there is a twofold relationship in intervals to be remembered: The distance between the two feet, and the distance between the last note played by one foot and the next note to be played by that same foot.

Praetorius

It will be seen that the right foot has only two notes to play, with the toe never leaving F and heel taking only the note below. The left foot must "think" the distance between B flat, C, and A.

While the bass line in example is given as a single line, in the hymnal there will always be a tenor line written above it. In marking pedaling this sometimes causes trouble since marks for the right foot pedaling actually appear above the tenor notes, causing the inexperienced organist occasionally to attempt to play the tenor note instead of the bass. It is generally understood that the mark Λ above the score is for the right toe; below the score, for the left. The marks O or U indicate the heel, left or right depending on its placement. When the same note is given for tenor and bass, the note is played by a foot as the bass and by the left hand as the tenor. This is done to keep the individual vocal lines well defined and clear in the organist's mind. (It will soon be discovered in playing hymns that the tenor line gives much more trouble than the bass.)

It should be understood that all bass notes are

played as written—not an octave below—unless the alteration is used for a roving bass line or the full sound of the pedal is inadequate. Do not be a "one legged organist," with the right foot glued to the swell pedal.

There are several fundamental pedaling actions and patterns which, when thoroughly understood, will help solve practically any pedaling problem.

1. White note to white note—the sidewise ankle movement.

Note particularly starting on G with the heel so that at the top of the line the toe is pointing away from the center of the pedal board. If possible, avoid ending on a distant note with the heel. The concave-convex principle of the standard pedal board calls for the toes to reach out toward the highest and lowest notes.

2. White note to black note—the up and down ankle movement.

9

Germany

Watch carefully for the difference between half steps and whole steps. (The distance between C and B flat, and E and F sharp is deceptive and is often missed.)

3. Alternating feet. Many hymns of the psalm tune or chorale type call for this treatment.

St. Anne

4. Thirds—and occasionally fourths—played by one foot. These are played with the foot at about a forty-five degree angle with the big toe playing one note and the heel the other. The note, or notes, skipped will then fall silently under the arch in front of the heel. Some teachers call this playing on the inside of the foot.

Cwm Rhondda[1]   St. Theodulph

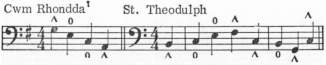

[1] By permission of W. Paxton & Co. Ltd., London.

10

Winchester Old

5. Slides from black to white by one foot. This is often necessary to make white-note scale patterns which follow a black note easier to play.

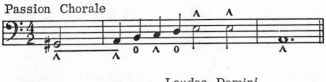

Passion Chorale

St. Thomas   Laudes Domini

A line drawn above or below helps to remind the player of the slide.

6. Slides from one black note to another. These occur most frequently in hymns in the keys of E flat and D flat major.

Dundee (French)   Diademata

Lancashire

11

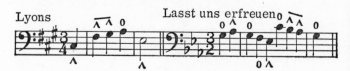

The first note is played with the outer half of the foot and the second with the inner half—or vice versa depending on the direction of the scale. When there are three black notes in a row the leading foot always plays the first two notes and the other the third.

7. Crossing the feet.

Ordinarily the left foot stays back and the right stays forward.

8. Substituting one toe for the other while holding a note. This should be done with a sense of rhythm—either on a main pulse or a subdivided beat.

Nun danket

Substitutions should be used *only* when there is no other solution. Many problem pedalings are solved by lifting the foot completely at the end of a phrase —where the music breathes and a lift is possible— and starting the next phrase with the same foot.

St. Hilda

These eight patterns represent the various pedaling actions commonly encountered in hymn playing, but no hymn is made up exclusively of any one given pattern. Rather, every hymn has its own idiosyncrasies which make it vitally important that the pedaling for each be studied and marked. Regardless of the patterns played, the foot movements should be quiet and unobtrusive, with the knees comfortably close together and the feet gliding over the keys. Many times the feet will seem to move along parallel with each other so that each is ready to help the other out of any difficulty.

One final warning: Do not let either foot wander, dangle aimlessly, or hang on the bench crosspiece while it is not in use. Keep the foot over the note it has just played until it moves with purpose to the next note to be played.

In order to give the student a clearer view of how these rules are applied to the total pedaling of a hymn, several hymn tunes are given with suggested markings.

Italian Hymn (Trinity)

Old 100th

Hyfrydol

Easter Hymn

Cwm Rhondda [2]

Dundee (French)

St. Peter

[2] By permission of W. Paxton & Co. Ltd., London.

17

Duke Street

CHAPTER II

Articulation and Touch

Good hymn playing is not entirely a matter of playing as the spirit moves one; a foundation of sure technique enables the spirit to move with more effectiveness. The following rules regarding repeated notes is as essential to the successful playing of hymns as it is to the playing of individual voices of a fugue.

1. Repeated notes in the soprano line are always broken to half their unit of value—not necessarily half of the value of the note. Thus two repeated quarter notes are played as follows:

With a half note followed by two quarter notes, such as the beginning of "Fairest Lord Jesus," a dotted quarter note followed by an eighth note rest is the solution.

St. Elisabeth

Care should be given to making the time values of the rests accurate, for most organists tend to hold the note too long and to cheat the rest. Since the only way to create accent and rhythmic stress at the organ is through the contrast of silence and sound, observance of rests and meticulous release of notes are of prime importance to clear, rhythmic playing.

2. Repeated notes in the bass line are broken on the same principle of the unit of value, but whether to break or not is determined by a study of rhythmic and harmonic design. Repeated notes over the bar line are always broken without exception because of the need for rhythmic impulse.

St. Anne

In any given measure repeated notes are broken if doing so adds to the life of the hymn.

Austrian Hymn

Aurelia

Lyons

In harmonically static passages the breaks are determined either by the change in chord or by some rhythmic characteristic inherent in the music. For instance, in the tune "Lancashire" the bass should be played as follows:

Lancashire

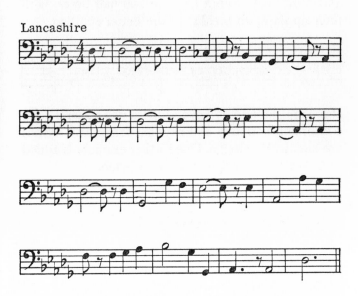

In the first measure of "Hymn to Joy" the question must be decided which of the following patterns is preferable (a) or (b):

a. Hymn to Joy

21

b.

The first gives a smooth quality; the second is perhaps closer to Beethoven's treatment in the symphony and gives an infectious drive to the tune. In the third phrase the harmonic movement on the first and third beats would indicate two half notes, with their appropriate breaks, as the better solution.

Hymn to Joy

It is impossible to go beyond these two general rules concerning harmony and rhythm, for no two hymns are identical in design. One further example is added to indicate the total pattern for a hymn.

Olivet

3. Repeated notes in the alto and tenor may generally be tied together except where more rhythm is

22

needed or clarity is necessary in the inner voices.

Ratisbon

If a congregation sings sluggishly, more and more detached playing is necessary, with repeated notes and sometimes whole chords broken. Some teachers recommend breaking soprano and alto, others soprano and tenor, and others soprano and bass.

Hursley

4. The beginning of a phrase on an upbeat usually calls for a complete break of half of the note value.

Irish

This creates a springboard which successfully launches the congregation into the hymn. After the hymn is under way it may not be necessary to detach all voices for upbeat chords unless all notes are repeated over the bar line.

5. At phrases with feminine endings—those in which the last note falls on a weak beat—the minimum of broken notes and rhythm is the rule, and the endings should be smooth and yielding.

Munich

6. As a general rule both hands and feet should be lifted at the end of each musical phrase, at the places where the congregation takes a breath. This pause, or break, takes one half of a pulse and must be subtracted from the last note of the ending phrase note so the forward movement is not halted.

Occasionally, as in "Nicaea," there is a need for a break or breaks before the end of the first musical phrase. In fact, "Nicaea" represents one of the trickiest of all hymn tunes to articulate carefully.

Nicaea

(a)

last phrase

(b)

Note the use of detached chords at (a) and (b) to keep cadences from becoming sluggish.

If all hymn texts and tunes coincided exactly as to phrase endings the organist's job would be simple, but such is not the case. For example, in singing "Faith of our fathers!" (St. Catherine) the organist—and congregation—should observe the exclamation point after "fathers" with a firm break and should then proceed to the end of the line without further

25

breaks—"living still in spite of dungeon, fire, and sword." But what should one do with this?

These things shall be: a loftier race
    Than e'er the world hath known shall rise
With flame of freedom in their souls
    And light of knowledge in their eyes.

Common sense says it is impossible for a congregation to sing from "a loftier race" to the end without a breath. In cases of this sort it is best for the organist to expect the congregation to breathe at the end of each phrase although he minimizes releases—or even omits them—in order to draw their attention to the continuity of thought.

7. All attacks should begin cleanly with hands and feet starting simultaneously. Many organists have a bad habit of putting down either the pedal note or the left hand first. Releases should likewise be clean, with no dangling pedal bourdons. Have your best friends listen and tell you.

8. Articulation and touch are affected and partially determined by the acoustics of the room, the way the congregation sings, and, most important of all, the form of the hymn. In a very reverberant and "live" room a nonlegato touch is absolutely necessary to achieve clarity; otherwise the chords tend to run into each other. In a "dead" room—one with little or no reverberance, due perhaps to too many carpets, draperies, and use of acoustically absorbent tile—the more legato style is necessary since each sound tends to die almost as soon as it is sounded. If the congregation tends to be sluggish in singing, non-

legato playing will help to create more vitality and move the congregation along at a crisper pace. While hymn patterns will be discussed in greater detail in another chapter, the following example may indicate the importance of relating touch to the form and design of a hymn:

Lobe den Herren

"Lobe den Herren" is fundamentally made up of a vigorous opening pattern—later appearing in the form of three repeated D's at the climax of the hymn —and a series of scales. This design can best be delineated by detaching the manual chords in the opening notes against a legato pedal.

In playing hymns listen for accuracy in note and rest values, for therein lies rhythmic control. But listen just as carefully for the right kind of touch, for therein lies rhythmic life and the pattern of the hymn.

CHAPTER III

Introducing the Hymn

Many organists play over a hymn tune before the congregation starts singing as if it were a matter of small or no importance—an unpleasant duty to be got through as quickly as possible. Yet, the introduction is a most important factor in good hymn singing.

The first job of the introduction is to give the correct tempo. (See the next chapter for a discussion of tempos.) The speed should be determined in the mind of the organist before he plays a note and should not vary between the introduction and the singing of the first stanza. Particularly to be avoided is a ritard or rallentando at the end of the introduction since this interjects a note of doubt in the singers' minds just as their confidence has been built up. Any uncertainty or unsteadiness courts disaster in the singing.

The introduction also gives the rhythmic design of the hymn—the shape of the tune. If the organist wants the congregation to sing the first few chords of "Lobe den Herren" with vigor, he must play the chords detached in the playing over as well as in the various stanzas. The entire style and mood of the hymn can be delineated by the proper tempo, touch, and organ tone. This means that the introduction should not be played on quiet flutes or a solo stop, even if the stops are beautiful. For an opening hymn of praise a full diapason chorus is possible and desirable—perhaps even including mixtures—with matching pedal reed. On a quieter hymn a diapason

8′ and 4′ may be adequate, and the pedal may be omitted for the introduction. There should, however, be no room for doubt in the singer's mind as to how the hymn should be sung when he begins.

The melody, of course, is presented in the playing over and should be articulated with extreme care, making sure that all repeated notes in the soprano are treated accurately and carefully. If the melody is not overly familiar to the congregation it is a good idea to play the entire hymn through, the melody only in octaves—the left hand doubling the melody in the right. Or if a good trumpet stop is available the melody can be soloed on a separate manual, with the left hand playing the alto and tenor parts and the feet the bass. If the melody is very familiar specialized treatment is not necessary, and it may even be advisable on a long hymn to make a cut—using perhaps the first and last phrases if this is harmonically and melodically feasible. *The Brethren Hymnal* [1] uses a unique method of small symbols above the scores to indicate satisfactory instrumental introductions when shortening is desirable. If an abbreviation is made, be sure that the tune is familiar, the tempo is clear, and that the final chord is the tonic. Many hymns modulate to a related key at the end of the first phrase or first half and ending there leaves the listener in doubt as to whether the organist is going to continue with the tune or expects the congregation to start singing. Another hymn type which creates confusion is represented in "National Hymn" with its trumpet fanfare. (See also "Victory"

[1] Elgin, Ill.: Brethren Publishing House, 1951.

with its alleluias.) It is best to start the introduction in measure three, omitting the opening fanfare; otherwise the congregation, not having sufficient time to get organized, may be panicked into starting the first stanza without being ready. In the early Lutheran tradition it was customary to play a "choralvorspiel" which meant a short improvised or written-out prelude on the chorale to be sung. Bach's "Orgelbüchlein" is a collection of such material.

At the conclusion of the introduction the organist has the opportunity of setting a pattern of the amount of time which will be allowed between all stanzas of the hymn. There is no exact, unvarying amount of time which is applicable to all hymns. One which ends on the third beat of a 4/4 measure presents a different problem from one which ends on the downbeat of a 4/4 measure. In "Joyful, joyful we adore Thee" ("Hymn to Joy") the last half note should receive more than two beats, probably three; while "Holy, holy, holy! Lord God Almighty" ("Nicaea") will end with three pulses and the breath on the fourth. If an organist is sensitive to the singing of the congregation and if he will sing the hymns quietly to himself he will have little or no difficulty in deciding what is a comfortable breathing time between stanzas and will invariably give the same amount for any given hymn.

Once the introduction is over and an opportunity for a good breath is given, the hymn should begin with dispatch and certainty. Both hands and feet should begin simultaneously—no playing the melody note first, holding down a pedal, or, as seems to be

30

the case in many English churches, sustaining the opening chord for a beat or so until the congregation decides to begin. Until a congregation and organist have "come to an understanding with each other," there may at first be some slight discrepancies between the two in the first measure or so. But if the organist plays with a sense of progression which passes through various chords and cadences to the climax of the hymn the congregation will soon trust his judgment and will begin with as much vigor and readiness as the organist displays in his playing.

CHAPTER IV

Tempos

It is hardly surprising that organists cannot agree on a "correct" hymn tempo when hymnal editors cannot do so either. Several hymnals have attempted to indicate an approximate speed and style by the use of such words as "majestically," "moderately"—this is used quite often as safe, middle of the road—"triumphantly," "with movement," and "with dignity." When "devotionally, in moderate time" appears, just what is really intended? Does not one feel a bit self-conscious when asked to play and sing "devotionally" or "with dignity"?

Two hymnals, *The English Hymnal* and *The Christian Science Hymnal,* are more specific and give metronomic markings. James Rawlings Sydnor in *The Hymn and Congregational Singing* [1] also indicates metronomic speeds at which he plays various hymn tunes. It is interesting to note the extremes of markings by these three for "Ein' feste Burg": (1) 40 to the pulse, (2) 69-76, (3) 80-88. The latter speed is actually twice as fast as suggested by *The English Hymnal.* A rate of 40 pulses to the minute means that it would take over eight minutes to sing "A mighty fortress," with Amen! Surely American congregations would not abide this.

Why the disparity? Obviously the British editors thought in terms of the cathedral, with sounds weaving their way back and forth through the long nave. Where the reverberation time is above four seconds

---

[1] Richmond, Va.: John Knox Press, 1960, p. 118.

such a slow tempo might be acceptable, but in practically every other situation a faster speed is desirable.

The Christian Science Hymnal editor points out: "For various reasons, there is never a fixed speed (tempo) for any piece of music, not even that indicated by the composer. Eminent editors and conductors show, in their markings and interpretations of standard compositions, decided tempo variations." [2] To illustrate, note the various markings (in order) for four tunes as found in (1) *Service Book and Hymnal*, (2) *Songs of Praise*, (3) *The English Hymnal*, (4) *The Hymnal* (Presbyterian, U. S. A.), and (5) *The Christian Science Hymnal:*

"Nicaea": (1) Joyfully, with dignity; (2) Very slowly—for first two measures, then "slightly faster"; (3) 42-50; (4) with exaltation; (5) 88-96

"Ein feste Burg": (1) Broadly, with vigor; (2) Very slow and solemn; (3) 40; (4) In majestic style; (5) 72-80

"Lobe den Herren": (1) Majestically, with movement; (2) Moderately slow; (3) 80; (4) Majestically; (5) 84-92

"Leoni": (1) With spirit; (2) With vigor; (3) 84; (4) Majestically; (5) 88-96

The correct tempo for one building or one congregation may not be right for another. The correct tempo for a given place and occasion must finally be decided upon after a study of the following factors:

1. The music period from which the tune came and the style of the composition. Plainsong calls for

[2] P. 617.

a speech rhythm—which will probably be faster in English than in Latin. A folk tune will invite a brisk tempo suggestive of freedom and high spirits. A hymn tune of the English cathedral school calls for more breadth of treatment than a "gospel" hymn tune. A chorale may be exuberant, as "Praise to the Lord, the Almighty"; meditative, as "Jesu, Priceless Treasure"; or forceful, as "A mighty fortress." Further, do not play chorales too slowly, and do not play "gospel" hymns too fast. Martin Luther was by no means a lethargic man, and to make all chorales "solemn" and "noble" is to mistake the temper of the times which created them and the style in which they were originally sung.

2. The phrase lengths as indicated by the metrical pattern. Short meter (S.M. 6.6.8.6.), common meter (C.M. 8.6.8.6.), and similar patterns having short phrases should be sung more deliberately to give them balance and dignity. Long patterns such as 10.10.10.10. must move more rapidly to make the phrases comfortable to sing on one breath. Long meter (L.M. 8.8.8.8.) hymns pose a peculiar problem since every phrase is of equal length—eight syllables. If all of the notes are also of equal length (see "Melcombe") the congregation will feel breathless if sufficient time is not given at the end of the second and fourth phrases for a comfortable breath. It is for this reason that the hold sign ($\frown$) is usually placed over these notes. (For further discussion of the hold sign see page 39). The long meter "Doxology" is much easier to sing in the original meter for the simple reason that the movement is balanced with points

of repose in the longer note values which begin and end the phrases. It can therefore be sung at a faster tempo than the even note method without a sense of being hurried or pushed.

Old Hundredth

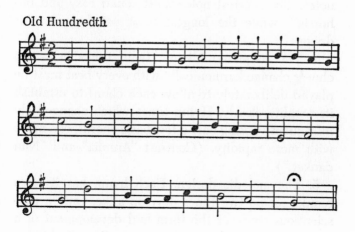

The thought structure of individual lines and the breath supply should always come out together evenly and comfortably.

3. The balance of long and short note values. Any hymn which ranges from whole notes down to eighth and sixteenth notes is difficult to pace because of the wide variety of rhythmic patterns. "What a Friend we have in Jesus" ("Converse") always gives trouble for the simple reason that the opening measure has a frantic fistful of notes, while the last note of the fourth measure is a whole note. The organist may be inclined to speed up the eighth notes too much to keep the long notes from seeming endless; the congregation is inclined to shorten the whole note— probably because the breath supply is gone—and to

move on to the next line. If a choice must be made, it is preferable to shorten the whole note. Another tune with the same basic problem is "Finlandia" with its rapid movement followed by slurred and tied notes. The shortest notes must sound easy and unhurried, while the longest must not feel slow or draggy.

4. The harmonic idiom. Hymn tunes in which chords change harmonically with every beat must be played deliberately to allow each chord to establish its tonality clearly. Hymn tunes which change only infrequently, using only a few basic chords, can move with more rapidity. (Contrast "Aurelia" and "Nun danket.")

5. The melodic design. Each hymn has its own tempo, for no two tunes develop alike. Only a conscientious study of the form and development of a tune will reveal its problems as well as its hidden beauties. And of course the words make each stanza a new problem. (For further help see Chapter 5, "Hymn Forms.")

6. The age and sex of the singers. Children will wish to sing hymns faster than their grandparents, and a group of men will not move along quite as rapidly as women.

7. The weaknesses of a tune. If a tune has poor points, the organist—if he must play it—should attempt to hide them and to make the tune sound as good as possible. Patterns of the dotted eighth and a sixteenth in most gospel hymn tunes should be smoothed out toward the triplet pattern so the rhythm is given as much stateliness and dignity as

possible. An organist, despising such inferior music, may be tempted to overaccentuate the negative points in order to show his annoyance—try "Toplady," exaggerating the dotted figures—but such a procedure is not the way to win the confidence of the congregation nor to educate them to better things.

In setting the tempo, play rhythmically and steadily—but not with deadly metronomic insistency—and work for the feeling of the long phrase and sweeping line. Many hymns with a fast 4/4 meter sound better and sing more easily in 2/2. (See "Duke Street," "Terra Beata," "Austrian Hymn," and "Hymn to Joy.")

There should be no obvious sense of ritarding at the end of any stanza except the last. Once a tempo is set by the organist and followed by the congregation nothing should be done to upset the forward impetus. Even the "Amen" should retain the vitality of the hymn and should be played and sung at the same tempo as the hymn. Some hymnals give two beats and others four for each syllable of the Amen, but whichever is used the organist should continue to count pulses and should release cleanly on an accent —i.e., third beat or downbeat in 4/4 time. A congregation at best is self-consicous about its singing, and if there is any insecurity created by uncertain stopping, tempo, beginnings of stanzas, or unexpected reharmonizations, what little confidence they have will be shaken, and the singing will deteriorate.

Playing the notes rhythmically and accurately is not enough, however. The good accompanist always plays the text. The tune usually associated with "O little town of Bethlehem" ("St. Louis") will sound quite wooden unless certain notes are dwelt upon momentarily where certain syllables are more important than those which precede them. For example, the syllable "Beth-" in Bethlehem must be given slightly more time than any other note in the first phrase. To exaggerate such a note will make a parody of the hymn tune, however, and a fine balance comes only with practice in singing the words while playing. Punctuation should be studied carefully, but the music should not be overpunctuated. A comma is not necessarily a flashing red stop sign. There are two kinds of commas: (1) a comma which indicates a separation, or break in thought, calling either for a breath or an infinitesimal breaking of the vocal line— "Immortal, invisible, God only wise"; (2) a comma which merely calls for a slight leaning on the previous syllable, such as "Be still, my soul."

As has been indicated previously, not all text phrases coincide with musical phrases; therefore, following the text mentally is of utmost importance. Many an organist has found himself playing an extra and needless chord at the beginning of the second stanza of "O come, all ye faithful"—"Sing, choirs of angels"—which begins on the downbeat instead of the upbeat to the measure. In a hymn such as "Where cross the crowded ways of life" or "Thou hidden Source of calm repose" where the last two stanzas are one sentence, the organist should reduce breathing time and plunge immediately into the final stanza so the congregation is carried along to the concluding thought and the climax of the hymn. Following the text will also prevent the embarrassment which many young organists have experienced of playing a fifth stanza for a four stanza hymn. Good hymn playing is primarily text playing.

The hold sign (⌒) is usually a problem to organist and congregation alike. It has come to mean a place where the congregation sits down vocally and mentally, thereby stopping the flow of the music. Particularly is this the case in chorales. Originally the hold sign served as a guide to the organist that the end of a phrase was passing. (See Bach's "Orgelbüchlein," where the under voices continue to move ahead while the soprano chorale note is marked with a hold. Obviously the hold does not mean to stop at all.) The sign was also used in organ literature to indicate a cadenza—always at some cadential point, where the organist was free to show his ability to improvise. In singing the chorales it should be clear that only at the cadential points should there be any real pause. For example, the first two phrases of "A mighty fortress" should be sung without any pause in the middle since the thought of the music and words have no reason to settle until the tonic cadence at the end. Likewise, in "Eisenach" there should be a pause only at the end of the second and fourth phrases, but not at the first and third.

"Luther" ("Nun freut euch") poses more of a problem because of the unusual grouping of three phrases which end the hymn. A possible solution is to allow one extra pulse at the end of the fifth and sixth phrases, making the note one beat followed by one pulse for breath.

Luther (Nun freut euch)

Most organists tend to treat holds at major cadences as if the note were two pulses followed by a rest on the third.

Melcombe

The principle involved here is that the rest should come on a pulse which is accented, thereby giving vitality to the breath and a bounce which carries the singer on to the next phrases. In some hymnals, such as *The Hymnal, 1940* and *The Hymnal for Colleges and Schools,* an attempted solution is made by writing out the note as a half note—implying one pulse singing, one pulse breathing.

In *The Methodist Hymnal* the tune "Irish" appears once with a hold at the end of the second phrase, and once without. Another C.M. tune, "St. Agnes," always appears with the final note of the second phrase tied over to another full measure. Obviously it is difficult to present in accurate notation what is comfortable at cadential points. Without a hold the ending is abrupt; with an added full measure the ending

40

is too long. Perhaps the hold is the answer, provided the organist is sensitive to the singing of the congregation and allows just enough time for a comfortable cadence but still manages to keep the hymn moving by thinking the long vocal line rather than the small phrases and motives.

Willan Swainson summed up the question of tempo in these words:

When the main impression left by a piece is that it sounds slow or quick, one may be sure that interpretation is radically at fault. . . . The right tempo for any piece of music is that which allows incident to unfold without hurry and without delay. And the way to discover the true tempo is not to approach music with prejudice towards the slow, the moderate or the quick, but to study the nature of a piece—its rhythmic impulses, its phrase relations, its interplay of accent, and the closeness of its harmonic texture. When an organist proceeds along these lines the question of speed generally resolves itself.[3]

[3] *Manual of Church Praise* (Edinburgh: The Church of Scotland Committee on Publications, 1932), pp. 206-7. Used by permission.

41

CHAPTER V

Hymn Forms

Hymn playing is an art—not a mechanical playing over of a tune four or five times. The organist, as an artist, must make as careful a study of the form of a hymn tune as he does the form of a Bach fugue. As an intermediary between the composer and the congregation he is responsible for guiding the interpretation, but he is also an intermediary between the creative thought back of the text and the spiritual worship of God by the people.

Although the organist may not be a composer, he cannot correctly interpret the tunes through his playing unless he understands something of the art of composing. And let it be clearly understood, writing a good hymn tune is one of the most difficult of arts, for a hymn tune must not only match the general mood of the entire hymn, it must also fit individual stanzas. Furthermore, while a hymn tune must be musically valid and creative, it should be within the ability of persons with limited musical training.

Before discussing the various factors which make a good hymn tune, we will examine some examples of poor tunes and note the lack of melodic invention and harmonic interest in the first:

Malvern

The monotony of rhythm in the second:

Campmeeting

And the lack of unity of purpose and goal in the third—every phrase has a different pattern:

Missionary Chant

In an informative series of articles in "The Choir" Francis B. Westbrook points out that a hymn tune is made up of "phrases and sentences," much in the same way as language.[1] The number of each is determined by the meter—e.g., common meter calling for four phrases—8.6.8.6. He uses the example of "Winchester Old"

[1] London (September, 1959; November, 1959; January, 1960; March, 1960).

Winchester Old

to show that the first phrase is called the announcing phrase and the second, the responsive phrase. Two pairs of these phrases make up a sentence. Each phrase ends with some sort of cadence—imperfect, or half, cadence; interrupted cadence; plagal cadence; and inverted cadence. Returning too often to the tonic key center at many cadences prevents the music from developing—or getting very far from home. Conversely, a tune which is constantly modulating to distant keys may break down any sense of tonality and cause confusion in the minds and ears of the congregation. For a study of good use of cadences see the following tunes: "Bremen," or "Neumark"; "St. Anne"; "Leoni"; and "St. Magnus." The longer the tune the more important the series of cadences becomes, for instead of four phrases—two announcing and two responsive—making one sentence, there may be two complete sentences or more. Some tunes are made up of "figures"—shorter rhythmic patterns which combine to make up a phrase.

Joanna

Often they are combined to make a sequence,

Richmond

but if overused become mannerisms and may invite parodying.

Dennis

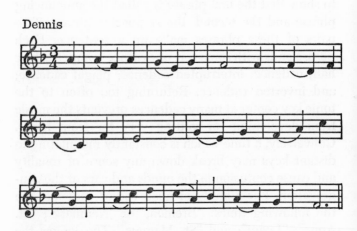

Even the longest tune can be broken down into its component parts with study, and letters are often used to indicate the general patterns:

"Joanna"—AABA

"Slane"—ABCD

"Cormac"—ABBA

"Lasst Uns Erfreuen"—AABBCCBBBBB

"Laudes Domini"—AABCCD

While all hymns have some basic phrase and sentence structure, the chief interest lies in how the composer handles the notes which constitute the various phrases. Interest is gained through melodic and rhythmic patterns. Contrast the opening phrases of two hymns:

Nun danket

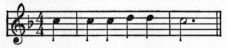

Leominster

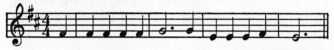

Notice how both use the principle of repeated notes, but how much more interesting the first tune is. Of course the harmonic treatment of "Nun danket" is a big factor. A good hymn tune must be able to stand on its melody alone, and the inventive composer seems to have some compulsion which, from the first note, pulls him toward the end of his journey. In "Laudes Domini" see how the first phrase gathers momentum to the top note, falls back slightly for another run to a higher note, then after riding the crest of the top D for three beats strides down to the cadential G. This is followed by a leaping pattern which is repeated verbatim—except for the harmony—then leaps upward in half notes to a ringing climax.

Laudes Domini

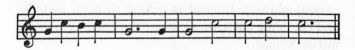

Or study "St. Bride" with its chordal minor pattern answered in the relative major, followed by a downward scale which seems to gather momentum and strength—a crescendo is obviously called for—before it resumes the opening leaping pattern starting on the highest note and plunging into the cadence.

St. Bride

Melodic invention and rhythmic patterns always go hand in hand. "Melcombe" and many other similar L. M. tunes are dull and difficult to sing with enthusiasm because they are composed of quarter note after quarter note.

Melcombe

"Old 100th," dull when sung with quarter notes, springs to life when the rhythmic variety of the original form is used. If a congregation objects to singing the original form of "Old 100th," have them sing "Abide with me" ("Eventide") with nothing but quarters to see how dull and monotonous it becomes.

Eventide

Some examples of tune beginnings which capture the interest immediately because of their successful use of varying note values can be found in "Lyons," "Lasst Uns Erfreuen," "Hyfrydol," "Irish," "Kremser," "Lobe den Herren," "Hendon," "Gräfenberg," and "Meirionydd."

The secret to the success of great hymn tunes lies in "their sense of vitality, progression and balance produced by the influence of duration, speed, and accent upon pitch." [2] Willan Swainson further stated:

The player who acquires a command over accent will never in hymntunes—and rarely elsewhere—have occasion to adopt more than an imperceptible variation of tempo. There are four important classes of accent— the metrical, the tonic (pitch), the agogic, and the cumu-

[2] *Op. cit.,* p. 202.

lative. The metrical, that which falls on the first beat of
the bar demands little attention here, since it already re-
ceives far too much in performance. The tyranny of the
bar line is nowhere more evident than in the rendering
of psalm and hymn tunes, where the habit of clubbing
the so-called "strong" beat of the bar on the head every
time it comes round has had far too long an innings.

Tonic, or pitch, accent is applied according to height.
A higher note does not necessarily carry an accent, but
simply a tendency toward accent. The context enables
one to decide.

Agogic accent is applied on the longer of two notes.
Here again length implies a tendency towards accent,
not an inalienable right.

Cumulative accent falls upon a note when its prece-
dents are so arranged as to give it special prominence.[3]

The latter is well illustrated by two tunes, "Benedic Anima Mea" and "Darwall's 148th."

Benedic Anima Mea

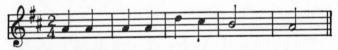

Darwall's 148th

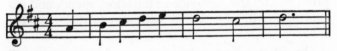

If the hymn tune is to be made clear in all its im-
plications the organist must look upon his job not as
an accompanist, following the whims and wishes of
the group; not as a leader, dashing ahead with the

[3] *Ibid.*, pp. 202-3.

bit in mouth, pulling madly at the dragging congregation; but as a conductor whose functions are

first, to inspire his forces, to set the mood and create
the atmosphere; second, to re-create the vitality of the
music—the energy and mobility of its rhythm, and its
sense of progression; and third, to indicate faithfully the
shape of the music—its melodic outlines, the significance
of its harmonic progressions, the relations of its phrases,
and the scale of its climaxes. The conductor, in short, has
three main concerns—the music's emotion, its life, and
its shape.[4]

[4] *Ibid.*, pp. 195-96.

CHAPTER VI

Registration

It is almost impossible to be specific in recommending organ registration for hymn playing since no two organs have the same stop-list, the same voicing, or the same size and type of space to fill. There are, however, certain definite principles which can serve as guides to the organist as he sits experimenting with various sounds.

1. The basic tone for leading hymns is the "diapason" or "principal."

2. Since the 8′ tone duplicates the pitch level of the singers, there should be more stops of pitch levels above the 8—4′, 2′, 2-2/3′, and mixtures (chorus mixtures first, and "sharp" mixtures only for added brilliance). The order indicated is the best for adding diapason stops. A flute 8′ can be substituted for the basis of a plenum registration, but the top pitch(es) should be principal tone.

3. Heavy, loud, oppressive, muddy, thick stops—often found in organs built in the early part of this century—should be omitted from the ensemble along with heavy 16′ stops which drag down the tone and pitch level. If the 16′ tone is light—such as a Quintaton—it may be added judiciously for hymns of a graver nature. If all the stops of an organ—16′, 8′, and 4′—are heavy and unpleasant, they sometimes sound better if played an octave higher, producing an 8′, 4′, and 2′ sound.

4. As a general rule avoid all 16′ couplers. They only add confusion to the pitch line and destroy transparency.

5. Only such stops as add to the ensemble should be used in full combinations. Flutes and soft strings added to diapasons merely muddy the tone and can only be heard if they are out of tune. Under *no* circumstances should a *voix celeste* or *unda maris* be included since these ranks are tuned sharp, or flat, and make the pitch line uncertain.

6. Use the minimum number of stops possible—piling on assorted sounds and invariably coupling the swell to great destroys clarity.

7. Use the reeds sparingly. Reeds at 16′, 8′, and 4′ pitch combine well with mixtures to give a fiery effect, but this should not be overdone. Reeds can be added to the full diapason chorus for climax on a final stanza of a hymn of praise.

8. Solo stops such as the clarinet, *vox humana,* oboe, et cetera, are not suitable for congregational accompaniment. If a melody is to be soloed to help guide the congregation on an unfamiliar tune, it should be played on trumpet stops against a diapason accompaniment.

9. Do *not* use the tremolo for congregational singing! Ever! Under any circumstances! A tremolo calls attention to itself by its wibble-wobbles and prevents the pitch from being steady and decisive. The tremolo may be useful once or twice a year with a solo flute or solo reed for the prelude.

10. Do not use full organ tone all the time. Organists' eardrums seem to become immune to loud sounds, but the congregation prefers support—not bombardment.

11. Do not underplay. Be sure the congregation

feels secure. When the building is bathed in tone the people will feel like diving in; when they fear they will be heard individually they will stop singing. An antiphonal division sounding from the rear of a very long and large sanctuary when coupled with the organ sound from the front is far superior to blasting the tone from one direction only. In the case of electronics additional speakers properly placed in front and rear help make it possible to fill the space with sound without overloading one or two small speakers in the choir loft.

12. Changes in registration in a single stanza should be rare and should never be made abruptly. For example, an organist may wish to reduce the organ before the last phrase of the last stanza of "Dear Lord and Father of mankind," but building up to fortissimo for "wind, and fire" and then dropping suddenly to pianissimo for "O still, small voice of calm" is overly dramatic and inartistic. Eric Thiman suggests, "Try to catch the mood and spirit of the poem as a whole, rather than indulge in word-painting of details." [1]

13. Changes in registration for various stanzas should be determined primarily by the text. Some hymns call for adding to the tone mass for each stanza with a climax in the last. Others may have the climax at some other point and end quietly. ("O little town of Bethlehem" ends with a prayer—obviously calling for a quiet ending.) Sometimes variety can be achieved through the use of differing tone quality—

[1] "The Beginning Organist" (London: Ascherberg, Hopwood & Crew, Ltd., 1954), p. 3.

diapasons for one stanza, chorus reeds and mixtures for another. Any variety, however, whether of quantity of volume or quality of tone, should be related to the hymn and should never be a matter of caprice.

14. Keep approximately the same volume level for the Amen. *Never* make a gradual diminuendo and rallentando. Amen means "so be it," so play the Amen as if you meant every word that was sung.

15. Pedal tone does not necessarily have to be used at all times. The pedal tone can be omitted for quiet stanzas, or only 8′ tone can be used to give the listener a rest from boom and bombast.

16. If the pedal has a good reed section, a praise hymn is effective with a diapason chorus—through mixtures—on the manuals contrasted with 16′, 8′ and 4′ reeds in the pedal. If there are no pedal reeds available, swell reeds can be added to the pedal through the swell to pedal 8′ and 4′ couplers.

17. The great to pedal couplers should not be added unless the pedal section is inadequate. In such cases, it is better to keep the swell, or choir, division uncoupled from the great but coupled to the pedal— at 8′ and 4′ pitches—to add clarity and fullness to the pedal ensemble.

18. If the organ is enclosed, open the shutters and leave them open.

19. Work out several different tutti, or plenum, combinations. For example, try a full diapason chorus, but with a 4′ reed instead of a 4′ diapason. Do not always use the same registration for every full hymn.

20. Unless the crescendo pedal has been adjusted to bring on only a clear full sound, leave it alone. If

16′ couplers come on plus everything in the organ ask the maintenance man to set up the crescendo pedal so it will bring on a clear ensemble.

21. Finally, have an assistant play different combinations while you listen to them from various locations in the building. An organist often is seated where he cannot accurately gauge the true sound of the organ. Be sure to hear yourself as others hear you.

CHAPTER VII

Variety in Hymn Playing and Singing

Since hymn texts are sung to a single tune, repeated over and over, there is often a tendency on
the part of the organist to be bored or the congregation to lose interest. In the previous chapter it was
suggested that variety in registration can be secured
through alterations in quantity of tone (degrees of
loudness) and quality of tone (various pitch and
color combinations).

The following devices can be used to stimulate and
to sustain interest—particularly in a long hymn of
many stanzas; but they should be used sparingly and
should encourage the congregation to sing rather
than call attention to the device as a gimmick. Carl
Halter warned:

They are not the substance of hymn playing. They are
spices, not food. They must be used as a great cook might
delicately use the most exotic condiments, but they must
not be offered as the meal. The danger in them is the
old and ever-present one that the music can so easily
replace God in the service. We remember a conversation
with a musically sensitive person who had attended a
service in a certain church. The organ, he reported, was
forever doing something. No hymn was played straight
through without variation; registration throughout the
service was extreme and dramatic; the choir jumped in
at all sorts of unlikely places. Our friend left the service
extremely conscious of the musician, but spiritually and
emotionally upset. That musician failed in that service,

THE ORGANIST AND HYMN PLAYING

because he showed the people himself, when they had come to see God.[1]

One of the simplest alterations is the addition of passing notes in the lower vocal lines. The Bach chorale harmonizations are an excellent example of how this can be done tastefully and musically. The organist must beware, however, lest he fall into the habit of adding passing sevenths at every possible oc-

Lobe den Herren

casion—particularly the cadence. Care should be taken that the additions do not change the harmony nor upset the person who is singing a part.

The "roving bass" is an extension of the idea of passing notes, and is effective in the psalter type of tune where the harmony lends itself to root positions and first inversions.

Laudes Domini

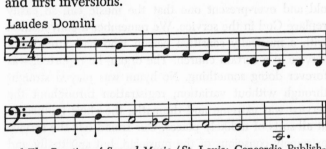

[1] *The Practice of Sacred Music* (St. Louis: Concordia Publishing House, 1955), p. 36. Used by permission.

58

St. Catherine (measures 17-20)

St. Anne

Ralph Vaughan Williams' powerful tune "Sine Nomine" gains much of its interest from the marching bass line. This driving quality can be underlined by adding the three opening notes of the tune to the bass of the last measure.

This, incidentally, gets the singing off to a better start at the first stanza. The single bass note is ineffective for setting the rhythm and establishing pitch.

"Sine Nomine," as it appears in many hymnals with a four part harmonization for selected stanzas, represents another method of securing variety—the alternation of unison and harmonized versions. If the hymnal does not indicate how stanzas are to be treated, announcement should be made by the minister orally or printed in the bulletin.

The free harmonization approach is effective if the congregation is forewarned; if a tradition for its use is established; if used infrequently—not more than once in a hymn, usually for the last stanza; and if the organist is skillful and prepares the new harmonizations in advance. (See the bibliography for helps and suggestions.)

Closely related to free harmonization is the use of faux bourdon—a version in which the melody is given to the tenor line, with the congregation singing the melody in unison, and a new harmonization provided giving new vocal lines to sopranos, altos, and basses. While a few of the more recent hymnals in America have included examples, most of the material available is published in England.

Descants are often used with hymn tunes, and are different from faux bourdons in that the descant is added above the tune without altering the harmony underneath. A sung descant adds brilliance to a festival service if the soprano line is well handled, but there is always the danger that the congregation will stop singing to listen to the descant, and this defeats the purpose of a hymn—to praise God. Perhaps more effective for most occasions is the playing of the descant on the organ. The organ tone merely increases the number of voices, the brilliance, and the texture when a fifth line is added, and the congregation will merely sense the added support and be encouraged to sing. On extremely rare festival occasions instruments might be used to play the descant—for example, a trumpet descant on "Christ the Lord is risen today" might be appropriate on Easter Sunday.

Some hymns with interesting inner voices lend themselves to playing one of the voices on a solo manual with tone which is slightly more prominent than the other parts or of a different timbre. For example, the tenor line of "Dominus Regit Me" is interesting enough to be soloed on another manual or even played above the soprano part. Sometimes the alto line can be played above the soprano—the two parts inverted to make the soprano part the lower voice; "St. Petersburg," by Bortnyanski is an effective example.

Canonic treatment—sometimes involving new harmonizations—is an effective device for occasional use. "Lasst Uns Erfreuen" has been arranged in many anthems as a canon, and a stanza could be played from the anthem copy. Or the canon can be played in octaves on pedal reeds, starting on the third beat of the first full measure. Some other tunes which have been treated canonically by composers in various settings are "Gräfenberg," "Tallis' Canon"—the canon can be soloed easily, "Mendelssohn," "Beloved," and "Foundation."

Many organists fall into the bad habit of playing an "interlude" between the last two stanzas of a hymn. While this device has a legitimate place in certain hymns and for certain times, its use for every hymn is inexcusable. For instance, in the hymn "Where cross the crowded ways of life," in which the last two stanzas are part of one long sentence, the organist should perhaps cut down the time between stanzas to move the thought pattern of the hymn along. To pause in the middle of a sentence for an interlude—which is often nothing more than a repeating of the final phrase—is to do violence to common as well as musical sense.

If an interlude is used, it should be a musical statement related to the hymn tune melodically and stylistically, which builds in tone and intensity and invites and encourages the congregation to sing the last stanza with added vigor and enthusiasm. If the hymn text has more than five or six stanzas, the interlude may be used to modulate up a half step for the final stanza—thereby calling for a little more energy and effort on the part of the congregation. Such modulations should be carefully thought out and practiced in advance of the service; otherwise they may be unmusical, ungrammatical, and uninspiring. If a hymn is printed in a high key in the hymnal, it may be wise to play all the first stanzas in a lower key and to reserve the high key for the final stanza. Needless to say, an organist should be able to play any hymn in any key; if at first it is difficult the modulations and transpositions can be written out.

Another use of the interlude—really an improvisation—is between stanzas of a relatively short hymn used for a processional or recessional. If more time is needed to get the choir into place without having to repeat part of the hymn, the organist can insert an improvisation for sixteen measures or so to provide the additional time, with the interlude appearing between the stanzas which seem best to permit the break without ruining the continuity of thought. For a festival of many choirs it is perhaps better to use two or more hymns rather than to insert interludes between all stanzas.

Still another possibility is the use of no organ at all—the hymn being sung without accompaniment. To organists this is a shocking suggestion, and it will be just as shocking to a congregation unless they are prepared for it. In some churches the device has worked well; in others it has met with resistance. The only guidance that can be given is to warn the congregation by announcement before the hymn begins which stanza is to be so sung and to be sure the choir gives added support and leadership in the singing.

In extremely long hymns some ministers have found it highly effective to have several stanzas read in unison and then follow with the singing of the final stanza. Some hymns lend themselves to being read, or sung, responsively—such as "Watchman, tell us of the night" and "Art thou weary."

The antiphonal treatment of hymns is of ancient usage with various treatments possible—men's voices and women's voices, choir and congregation, unison and harmony. Of course such treatments must be clear to everyone if they are to be successful.

With such a tempting smorgasbord of devices at hand, there may be a temptation to try a little of everything at once. The result can only be musical and spiritual indigestion. To use another figure of speech, the organist must keep these devices in proper perspective as only a part of hymn playing, and hymns as only a part of worship.

Coda

Finally, some words of advice from others who see the organist's task as "a ministry, not as a profession" and playing hymns as "a craft, not a bore."[1]

Willan Swainson:

A musician may have the best imagination in the world, but in the end that which he truly expresses will be what he has first impressed on his own mind and character. The organist cannot put on artistry with his gown on Sunday morning and throw it off at night. His kingdom of music is within him. His expression is the reflection first of what he is, and next of what he would be.[2]

Carl Halter:

It is in the area of taste and emotion . . . that the organist makes his chief contribution to hymn singing. He can by means of registration and tempo so clarify the meaning of the hymn and uncover its emotional drive that the congregation is, as it were, lifted beyond itself. This is an art which defies description and which cannot be achieved simply by following a set of directions, but it is an authentic and necessary part of service playing and one of the great values of hymnody.[3]

Eric Routley:

It is your duty, your contribution to the service, to interpret as well as to play. . . . You are taking those

---

[1] Eric Routley, "The Organist's Guide to Congregational Praise" (London: Independent Press, Ltd., 1957), p. 7.

[2] *Op. cit.*, p. 196. Used by permission.

[3] *Op. cit.*, p. 33. Used by permission.

words and notes out of the printed book and presenting them to the congregation as a *new*, fresh, contemporary thing. . . . Do nothing mechanically, by habit, or lightly, or casually. Do all by decision. Do all after thought and prayer. And may the beauty of the Lord our God be upon us, and may He prosper our handiwork.[4]

[4] *Op. cit.*, pp. 12-13.

Bibliography

Bairstow, E. C. *Organ Accompaniments to the Unison Verses of 24 Hymn-Tunes from the English Hymnal.* London: Oxford University Press. (M)*

Clokey, Joseph W. *In Every Corner Sing.* New York: Morehouse-Barlow Company, 1948.

Coleman, H. *Varied Hymn Accompaniments.* London: Oxford University Press. (M)

Conway, M. P. *Church Organ Accompaniment.* London: Canterbury Press, 1952.

Cronham, C. R. *How to Play Hymns.* New York: Harold Flammer, Inc., 1961.

Halter, Carl. *The Practice of Sacred Music.* St. Louis: Concordia Publishing House, 1955.

Hymnal, 1940, Companion, The. New York: The Church Pension Fund, 1949.

Lovelace, Austin and Rice, William. *Music and Worship in the Church.* Nashville: Abingdon Press, 1960.

Lutkin, P. C. *Hymn Singing and Hymn Playing.* Evanston: Northwestern University, Department of Church Music, Bulletin III, 1930.

Manual of Church Praise. Edinburgh: The Church of Scotland Committee on Publications, 1932.

Noble, T. T. *Free Organ Accompaniments to 100 Well-Known Hymn-Tunes.* Glenrock: J. Fischer & Brother. (M)

Routley, Eric. *The Organist's Guide to Congregational Praise.* London: Independent Press, Ltd., 1957

————. *The Music of Christian Hymnody.* London: Independent Press, Ltd., 1957.

Rowley, A. *Extemporisation.* London: Joseph Williams, Ltd., 1955.

Shaw, G. *The Descant Hymn-Tune Book.* London: Novello & Company. (M)

* M=music.

_____. *36 Descants with Accompaniment for use with the English Hymnal*. London: Oxford University Press. (M)

Stellhorn, Martin H. (comp.). *Index to Hymn Preludes*. St. Louis: Concordia Publishing House, 1948.

Sydnor, James R. *The Hymn and Congregational Singing*. Richmond, Va.: John Knox Press, 1960.

Thiman, Eric H. *The Beginning Organist*. London: Ascherberg, Hopwood, & Crew, Ltd., 1954.

_____. *20 Faux Bourdons*. London: Bayley & Ferguson, Ltd. (M)

_____. *Varied Accompaniments to 34 Well Known Tunes for Unison Singing*. London: Oxford University Press. (M)

_____. *Varied Harmonies to Hymn Tunes*. London: Oxford University Press.

_____. *Varied Harmonizations of Favorite Hymn Tunes for Organ*. New York: H. W. Gray. (M)

Whitley, W. T. *Congregational Hymn Singing*. London: Dent and Sons, Ltd., 1933.

INDEX

Hymn tune titles are identified by an asterisk (*).

Date Due